HOISTS, CRANES, AND DERRICKS

HERBERT S. ZIM
JAMES R. SKELLY

ILLUSTRATED BY GARY RUSE

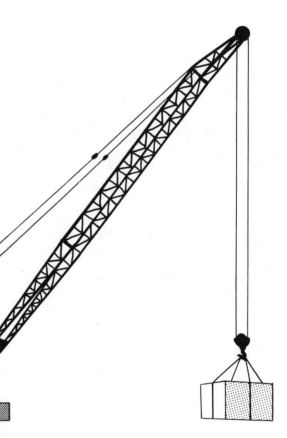

WILLIAM MORROW AND COMPANY NEW YORK

By the Same Authors
MACHINE TOOLS

A Rogewinn Book

5   75

When you want to lift something, you use the muscles of your arms, back, and legs. A few men, who have practiced lifting, can raise weights of 1500 pounds or so. With the help of machines people can lift more, and with power machinery, much more.

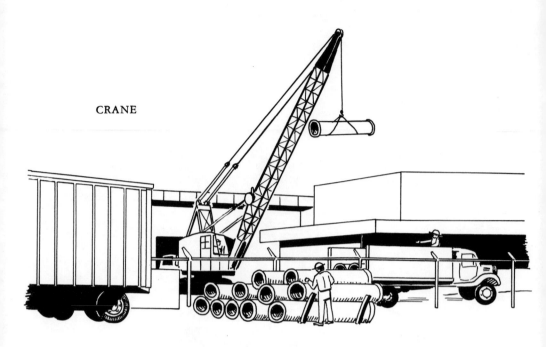

CRANE

In modern factories, at seaports, and in construction, heavy loads are lifted, moved, and piled by hoists, cranes, and derricks. You can see these important and sometimes breathtaking machines at work almost every day. But they are not a new invention. Long ago, before we have any records, men learned to use poles and vines for moving heavy things.

The first simple way of hoisting was to stand above a load and raise it by pulling on a vine or rope. Later men learned that they could lift a load by pulling downward on a rope that had been led over a branch or a smooth rock. This method was much easier.

ROMAN CRANE ABOUT 400 A.D.

The first practical lifting machines were built by the Romans only about 1500 years ago. They were cranes powered by slaves walking inside a treadmill. This treadmill looked like the exercise wheel of an animal cage. The slaves walked endlessly inside it, making it turn. The turning shaft of the wheel wound up the rope and slowly raised the load.

Modern hoisting machines now use a rope of fiber or steel strands. They also use pulleys and movable booms to make the lifting job easier and smoother. Instead of being powered by human muscles, however, they are run by gasoline, diesel, or electric power.

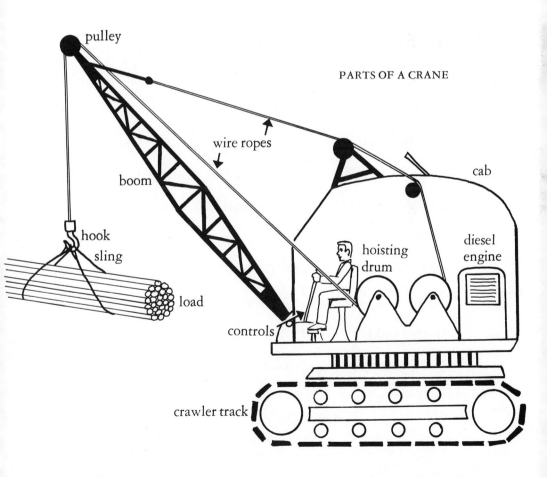

PARTS OF A CRANE

pulley
wire ropes
boom
hook
sling
load
controls
crawler track
cab
diesel engine
hoisting drum

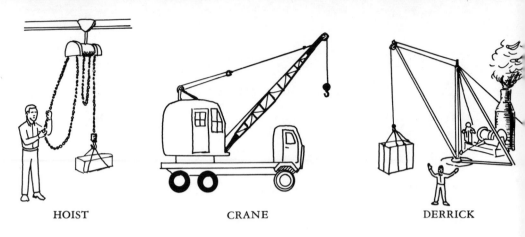

HOIST   CRANE   DERRICK

Lifting, or hoisting, machinery is of three types—hoists, cranes, and derricks. Hoists usually hang above the load from a girder or a set of rollers on an overhead track. When they hang on rollers they can be moved around.

Cranes are often mounted on trucks, railroad cars, barges, or crawlers. They are used to lift and carry the load from one place to another.

Derricks usually remain in one place. But they are often built so they can be taken apart easily, in a few days, and moved from one job to the next.

The ropes, pulleys and winches of hoisting machinery are called the rigging, just like those on old sailing ships. Ropes made of natural and man-made fibers and steel-wire cables are the very heart of hoisting machines.

PLANTS USED FOR ROPE FIBERS

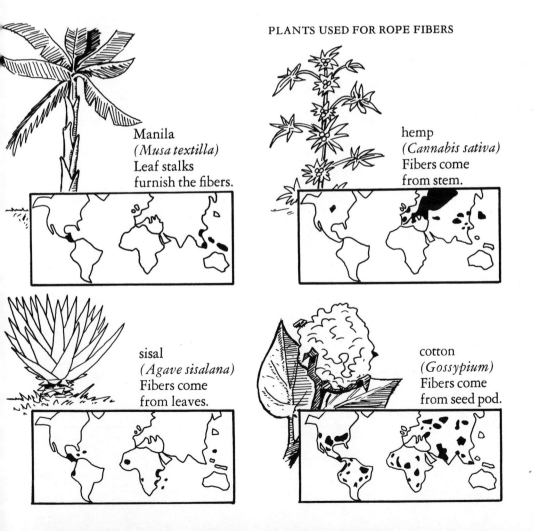

Manila
(*Musa textilla*)
Leaf stalks
furnish the fibers.

hemp
(*Cannabis sativa*)
Fibers come
from stem.

sisal
(*Agave sisalana*)
Fibers come
from leaves.

cotton
(*Gossypium*)
Fibers come
from seed pod.

The ropes used for the rigging of lifting machines are made of wire. They are much stronger and wear better than ropes made of natural fibers, like Manila, or synthetic fibers, like dacron. Each fine, tough wire runs from one end of the rope to the other. Thus the wire rope, or cable, has almost the strength of a steel bar of the same size. Chain is used to lift a load over sharp bends where a wire or fiber rope would be cut or worn.

kind of fiber	breaking strength of rope 1 inch in diameter	weight of 100 feet of rope
Manila	9,000 lbs.	27 lbs.
nylon	24,000 lbs.	25 lbs.
dacron	20,000 lbs.	30 lbs.
polyester	16,500 lbs.	31 lbs.
polypropylene	14,000 lbs.	17 lbs.
wire	79,000 lbs.	155 lbs.

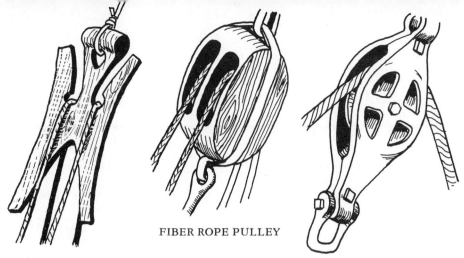

FIBER ROPE PULLEY

ANCIENT WOOD PULLEY   WIRE ROPE PULLEY

Pulleys change the direction of the pull on a rope. With them, the machine operator can pull an object from around a corner or lift something by pulling down. Pulleys have grooved wheels called sheaves, which hold the rope. Some pulleys have only one sheave; others have five or more.

Pulleys are often called blocks by people who work with them, because they were once carved from blocks of wood. Now many kinds of blocks are made. Each is used with its own size and kind of rope.

11

Pulling down on a rope that has been led over a pulley is much easier than pulling up. But still a fifty-pound pull is needed to raise a fifty-pound sack of flour. If the rope is passed through four pulleys, a boy can lift four sacks of flour (200 pounds) with the same fifty-pound pull, because there are now, in effect, four ropes pulling on the load.

However, the boy must pull longer to lift 200 pounds. To raise one 50-pound sack of flour one foot, the boy pulls one foot of rope.

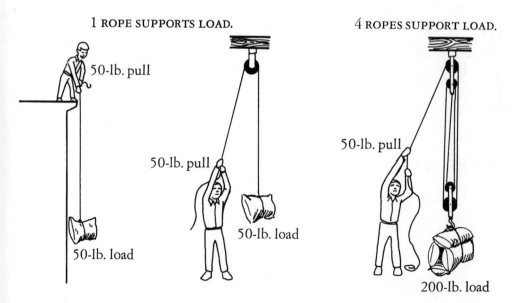

1 ROPE SUPPORTS LOAD.

4 ROPES SUPPORT LOAD.

50-lb. pull

50-lb. pull

50-lb. pull

50-lb. load

50-lb. load

200-lb. load

To raise 200 pounds of flour one foot, the boy must pull four feet of rope. The work is not less, but it is easier. He can pull 50 pounds four feet more easily than he can lift 200 pounds one foot.

This arrangement of pulleys gives the boy a mechanical advantage. Mechanical advantage is the relation of the pull or effort to the load. When a 50-pound effort lifts a 200-pound load, the pulleys provide a mechanical advantage of four, which is the same as the number of ropes supporting the load. By using more pulleys, and different combinations, the mechanical advantage can be increased. On hoisting machines the number of ropes (called parts) may vary from one to eight or more, each giving a different mechanical advantage.

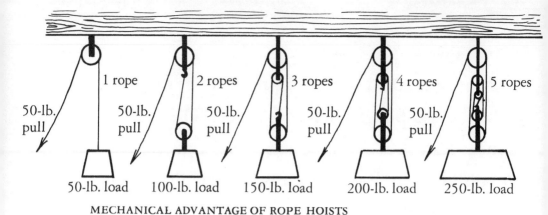

| 1 rope | 2 ropes | 3 ropes | 4 ropes | 5 ropes |

50-lb. pull   50-lb. pull   50-lb. pull   50-lb. pull   50-lb. pull

| 50-lb. load | 100-lb. load | 150-lb. load | 200-lb. load | 250-lb. load |

MECHANICAL ADVANTAGE OF ROPE HOISTS

HOISTING ENGINEER QUIZ

1. How much pull is needed to raise a 300-lb. weight with a 3-part hoist?

2. A man lifts a 100-lb. load with a 4-part hoist instead of carrying it up on his back. How much less effort does he make?

3. A winch can lift 3 tons safely. What kind of a hoist is needed so it can lift a 10-ton load?

4. You can use either a 2-part hoist or a 4-part hoist to lift the same load. Which is the faster?

5. One man lifts a 500-lb. weight with a 5-part hoist; another lifts a 300-lb. weight with a 3-part hoist. Which works the harder?

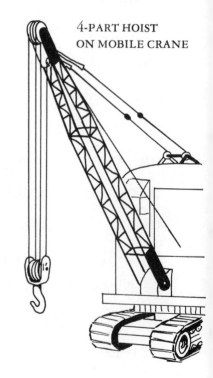

4-PART HOIST ON MOBILE CRANE

ANSWERS

1. 100 lbs 2. ¾ as much 3. 4-part hoist 4. 2-part hoist 5. Both make the same effort.

To pull the ropes and cables of modern hoisting machines, a winch often is used. Large winches have a pull of many tons. Whatever the size, each winch has a reel or steel drum, which winds up the wire rope. The drum is attached to a strong steel shaft, which is turned by a gasoline or diesel engine, or by a powerful electric motor.

The engine or motor is connected to the winch by gears that control speed and power. The strong steel base of the winch is bolted to the frame of the lifting machine. Both the base and the bolts must be strong enough to stand the pull of the load.

A brake band runs around one end of the winding drum of the winch. Made of strong spring steel, it tightens quickly when the operator pulls a lever or steps on a pedal.

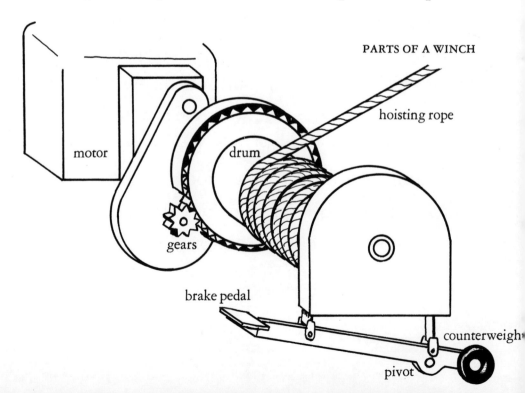

PARTS OF A WINCH

hoisting rope

motor

drum

gears

brake pedal

counterweight

pivot

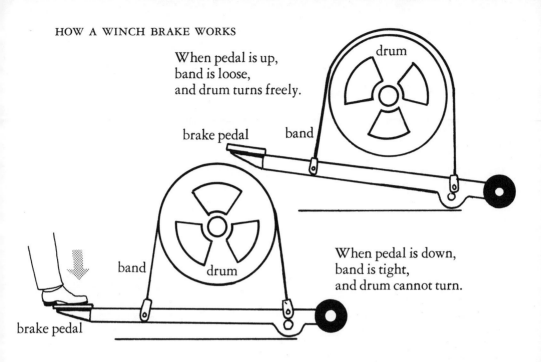

When pedal is up,
band is loose,
and drum turns freely.

drum

brake pedal   band

When pedal is down,
band is tight,
and drum cannot turn.

band   drum

brake pedal

Then the drum cannot turn. The brake must be strong enough to stop the drum quickly and hold any load that the machine is lifting. It must never fail.

The operator checks the winch every day to be sure all its parts are in good working condition. He sees that the winch and the engines are properly oiled and adjusted, so they will not burn out or be damaged in use.

17

Every hoisting machine must have power to turn the wheels, pull the ropes, and drive the winches. First, the muscles of slaves provided the power. Then horse power was used, and it lasted for hundreds of years. About 1760, horse power gave way to steam power, and later to gas, diesel, and electric power. Today we still use the term horsepower to measure the work done by machines.

HORSE-POWERED
DERRICK

STEAM-POWERED
CRANE

Modern engines are not only more powerful, they take up less space. This improvement is very important for hoisting machines, because many of them are self-propelled. Some have a separate engine to move the machine. A mobile crane is an example. Others, like a wrecker, may use the same engine for hoisting and moving around.

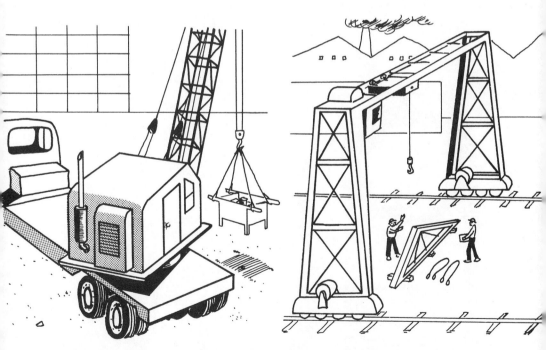

DIESEL-POWERED
MOBILE CRANE

ELECTRIC-POWERED
BRIDGE CRANE

Of the three types of hoisting machinery, the hoist is the easiest to use. The simplest form of the hoist is a pulley and rope, or a block and tackle, that can lift a ton or two. For heavier loads, mechanics and factory workers use gear-driven chain hoists powered by hand or by a small electric motor. These machines get their mechanical advantage from the gears inside the body of the hoist. Large electric chain hoists can lift as much as 25 tons, or 50,000 pounds.

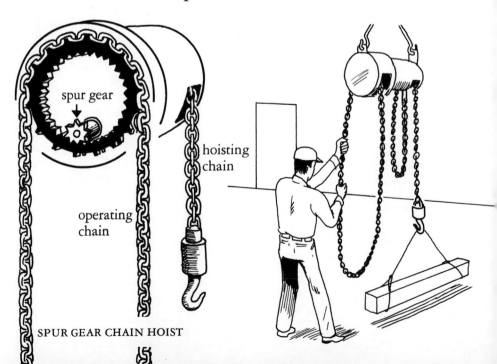

spur gear

hoisting chain

operating chain

SPUR GEAR CHAIN HOIST

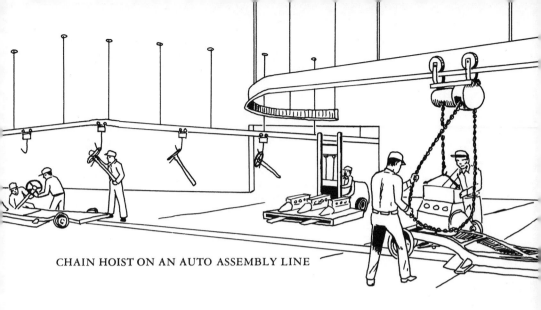

CHAIN HOIST ON AN AUTO ASSEMBLY LINE

A hand chain hoist has two sets of hanging chains. The one with a hook on the end lifts the load. The other is a chain loop. It turns the wheel that turns the gears that wind up the chain with the hook on it. This chain loop is called the operating chain. When the operator wants to raise the load, he pulls the operating chain one way. When he wants to lower the load, he pulls the operating chain the opposite way. In factories and shops, chain hoists often hang from tracks.

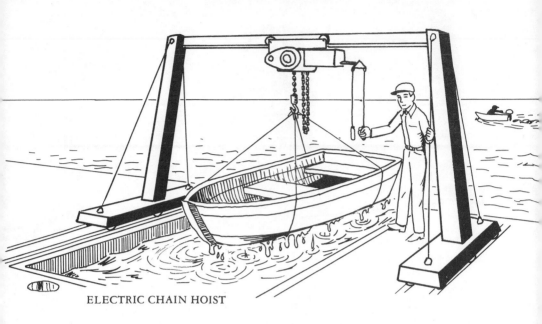

ELECTRIC CHAIN HOIST

Electric hoists are powered by motors. They are made with two ropes hanging down from a switch. Pull one to raise the load; pull the other to lower it. Some electric hoists have a small control panel hanging from the motor. By pressing buttons, the operator controls the speed, up-and-down movement, and sometimes the back-and-forth movement of the hoist. Hoists are used on assembly lines and many other places in factories.

Often hoists are made for special jobs, like placing the engine in a car on the assembly line. On such a hoist there is a hook that quickly and safely grabs the heavy engine and releases it when it is in place.

Usually a hoist does not have a special operator. It is used by the men on the job—the assembly-line workers, the mechanics, the repairmen. No special training or skill is needed. With an hour's practice—sometimes even less—most people can learn to operate the average hoist.

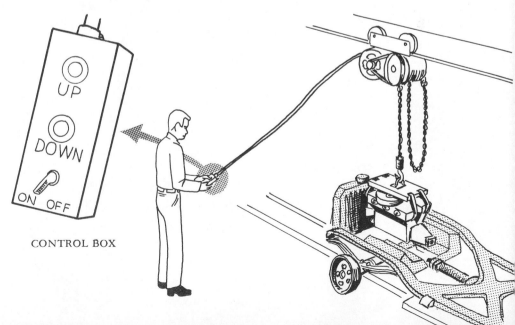

CONTROL BOX

Cranes are used for lifting heavier loads. They can pick up a load and move it for some distance before setting it down. Cranes are built in different ways for different uses. Some look like bridges or tall towers; others ride on large rubber tires or on railroad wheels and tracks. Some cranes have clamshells for digging; others have special hooks or slings for handling boxes or bags.

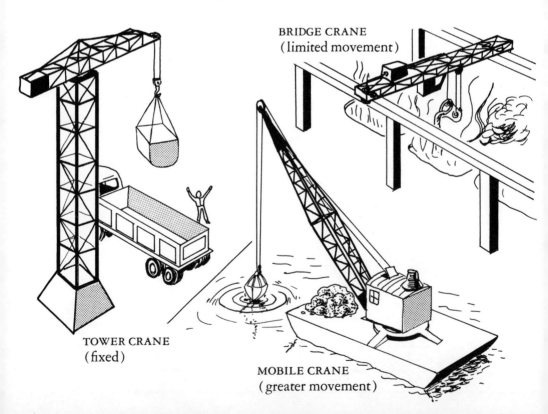

BRIDGE CRANE
(limited movement)

TOWER CRANE
(fixed)

MOBILE CRANE
(greater movement)

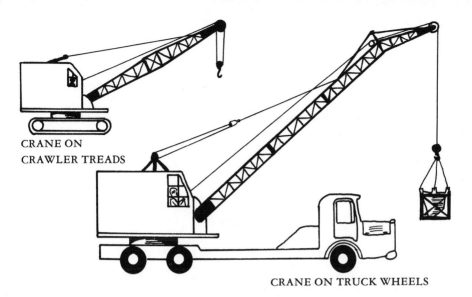

CRANE ON
CRAWLER TREADS

CRANE ON TRUCK WHEELS

The crane you most often see is the mobile crane. Its main parts are the undercarriage, the cab, and the boom. The undercarriage may be truck wheels, crawler treads, a railroad car, or even a floating barge. In the cab are the engine, the winch, and the controls that the operator uses to move the crane or to raise and lower the load. The boom is adjustable. Sections can be added or removed to make it longer or shorter. The operator's position gives him a good view of the job.

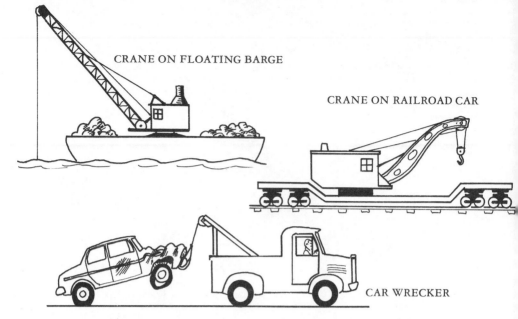

CRANE ON FLOATING BARGE

CRANE ON RAILROAD CAR

CAR WRECKER

Many different rigs appear on mobile cranes. Most common is the regular hoisting rig with a sling and a hook. A familiar example is the wrecker, with its short A-frame boom and light rigging. It raises one end of a disabled or wrecked car and tows the car back to the garage. There are also railroad wreckers, which construct and repair tracks as well as remove wrecks, and mobile cranes for driving foundation piling and other construction uses.

A number of different end tackles may replace the hook. One of the most common is the clamshell bucket, which is used for digging. With it, the mobile crane can dig in deep holes or underwater, where power shovels are useless. Each of the many other attachments serves some special purpose.

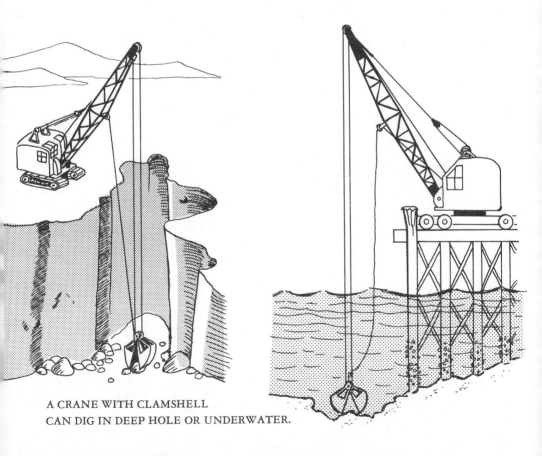

A CRANE WITH CLAMSHELL
CAN DIG IN DEEP HOLE OR UNDERWATER.

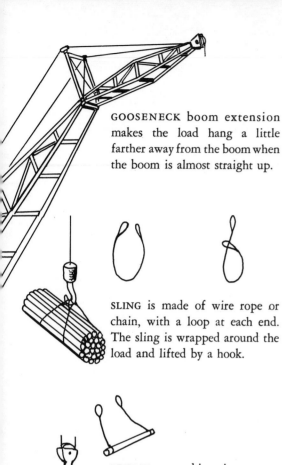

GOOSENECK boom extension makes the load hang a little farther away from the boom when the boom is almost straight up.

SLING is made of wire rope or chain, with a loop at each end. The sling is wrapped around the load and lifted by a hook.

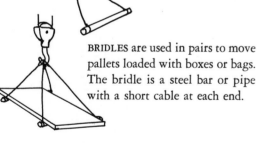

BRIDLES are used in pairs to move pallets loaded with boxes or bags. The bridle is a steel bar or pipe with a short cable at each end.

ELECTRIC MAGNET is used for lifting iron and steel in shipping terminals, junkyards, steel mills, warehouses, and factories.

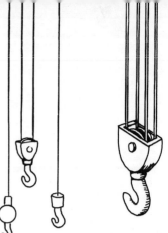

HOOKS may have blocks with one or more sheaves. A large iron ball often is carried above the hook to give it more weight.

TONGS are used to pick up large pieces that have irregular shapes, such as stumps, large boulders, or logs.

ORANGE PEEL is used for digging in broken rock, gravel, rubble, or other material when pieces are too large for clamshell bucket (p. 27).

GRAB is for moving larger pieces of broken material too large for the orange peel such as scrap iron, scrap lumber, or small boulders.

BOOM EXTENSION is bolted in the middle of the boom to make it longer, so it can reach higher.

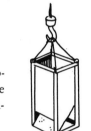

HAIRPIN is a bent steel bar used to pick up coils of wire, rolls of sheet metal, or other circular materials.

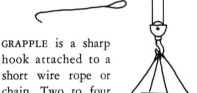

GRAPPLE is a sharp hook attached to a short wire rope or chain. Two to four grapples are used to lift crates or large pieces.

SKIP is a steel box with a trap-door on the bottom used to move gravel, limestone, or other granular materials.

SKULLCRACKER is a heavy ball of steel used to knock down wood or masonry buildings, walls, or other structures.

CONCRETE BUCKET carries concrete from mixer or truck to concrete forms on job. Workers open spout at bottom when bucket is in place.

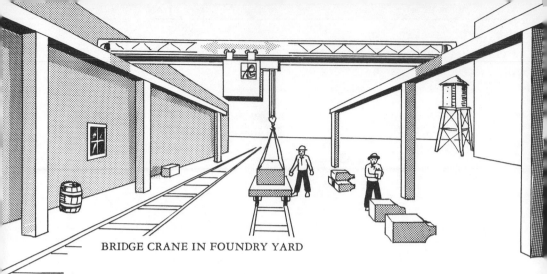

BRIDGE CRANE IN FOUNDRY YARD

The bridge crane reaches across a shop or storage yard like a bridge. It has wheels at each end that roll along tracks on both sides of the shop. Another set of rails runs across the bridge, and a trolley carries the hoisting machinery back and forth on them. With these two sets of rails, the crane reaches every part of the shop.

The operator of the bridge crane (sometimes called an overhead crane) rides in a cab. In some cases, the cab remains at the end of the bridge, and in others it is part of

the trolley. With levers and pedals, the operator can raise or lower the load, run the trolley back and forth across the bridge, or move
the bridge itself up and down the yard. The
crane has three powerful electric motors, one
for each of these jobs.

Bridge cranes are used to move steel ingots
in foundries or any heavy finished product to
the loading dock or onto flatcars.

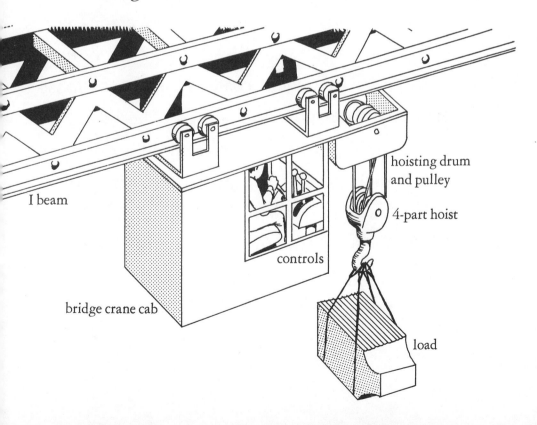

I beam

hoisting drum
and pulley

4-part hoist

controls

bridge crane cab

load

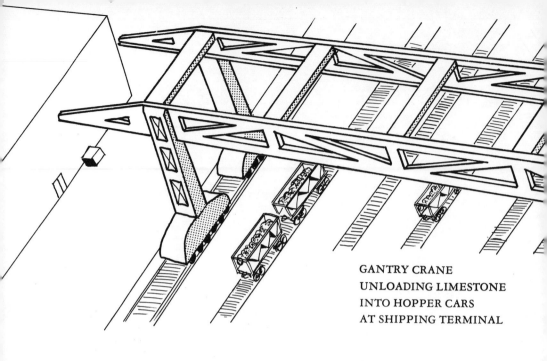

GANTRY CRANE
UNLOADING LIMESTONE
INTO HOPPER CARS
AT SHIPPING TERMINAL

The gantry crane is a bridge crane with long legs that are called gantries. It is used in large yards where coal, ore, or other loose materials are moved or stored. The bridge of some gantry cranes has balanced extensions that reach beyond the gantries so the trolley can run out farther. This kind of gantry crane is found along the waterfront, where cargo ships are unloaded.

The ship is tied up underneath the extension. Then the clamshell of the crane digs the coal or ore out of the ship's hold and carries it over to the storage piles or to a line of waiting railroad cars. The crane operator must be skilled enough to get all the cargo out of every corner of the ship. He must do the job without banging the heavy clamshell into the hatch, the crane, or the railroad cars.

The quay crane also runs along a dock or an unloading area in a port. It loads and unloads boxed or bagged cargo. This crane has no bridge. Instead, it usually is mounted on a single gantry that moves on a pair of dockside tracks. Atop the gantry is the boom and a small house, where the motors and winches that raise the load and the boom are located. At the front of the house is the operator's cab. The long boom, on the front of the crane, can be raised and lowered. Lowering it gives the crane a longer reach; raising it gives a shorter reach but a stronger lift for heavier loads.

Many of the world's ports are so planned that several quay cranes can work a ship at the same time. The quicker the cargo can be unloaded and a new cargo stowed aboard, the less the operation will cost the shipowners.

SOME KINDS OF QUAY CRANES

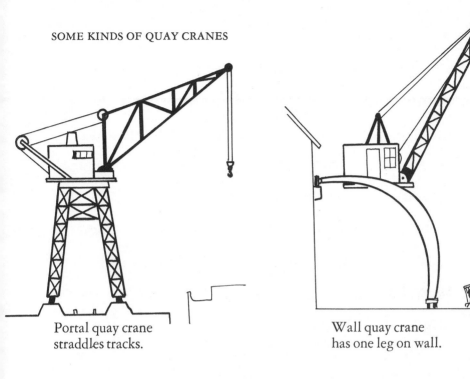

Portal quay crane
straddles tracks.

Wall quay crane
has one leg on wall.

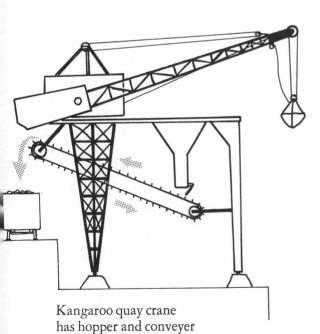

Kangaroo quay crane
has hopper and conveyer
to load cars.

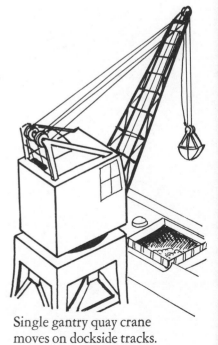

Single gantry quay crane
moves on dockside tracks.

The entire house and boom of the quay crane pivot on a large turntable that tops the gantry. Thus the crane can turn in any direction. At the back of the house, huge counterweights of concrete or iron are bolted to the frame. They keep the crane balanced when it picks up a load and rotates. All cranes that turn have counterweights to help keep them from tipping over.

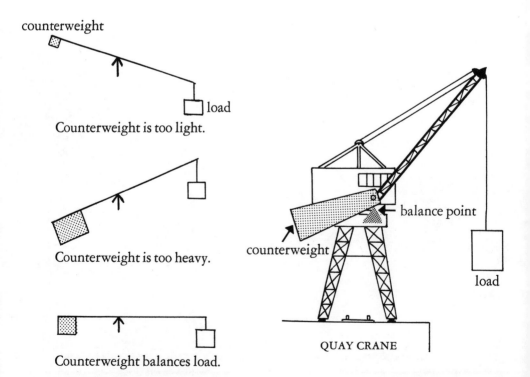

counterweight

load

Counterweight is too light.

Counterweight is too heavy.

balance point

counterweight

load

Counterweight balances load.

QUAY CRANE

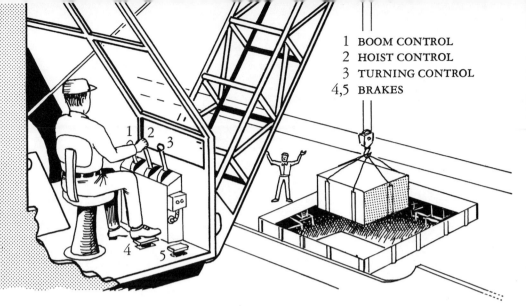

The controls to hoist and drop the load, to raise and lower the boom, and to turn the crane or move it down the track are located in the cab. The cab is placed high on the crane so the operator can see clearly, even when the hook is deep in the hold of a ship. The operator is very careful when he raises a load; he moves it skillfully and safely. Workmen and ship's crewmen always stand in the clear. They could be crushed if a cable parted or a load slipped from its sling.

37

The tower crane, like the quay crane, is used in shipyards and also in building construction. It is very tall, with a boom that sticks out from the top of the tower and reaches over the area where loads are picked up and set down. Tower cranes take up less space on the ground than quay cranes.

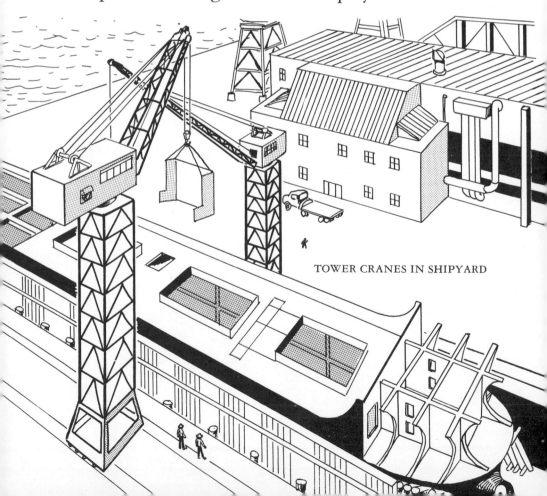

TOWER CRANES IN SHIPYARD

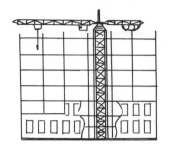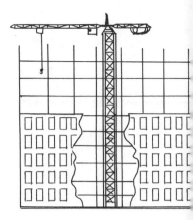

In shipyards, giant tower cranes run on rails. They move the large steel plates and beams that will be welded or riveted together to build new ships.

Tower cranes used in the construction of high-rise buildings are short at first. As the building gets taller, sections are added to the middle of the tower, making it taller too. The crane is often set in one of the elevator shafts of the building, so it can be raised as the building goes up. It carries steel, concrete, and other supplies to the workers on the upper floors.

Hammerhead cranes are tower cranes that have a trestle supported by cables attached to a strong mast. A trolley with a hoist runs back and forth along the trestle. Hammerhead cranes have a large lifting capacity and may be used to set a whole section of a ship in place at one time. The long trestle is balanced by the machinery house. The operator from his cab in the machinery house can reach a large area by turning the crane around on a pivot and ring atop the tower.

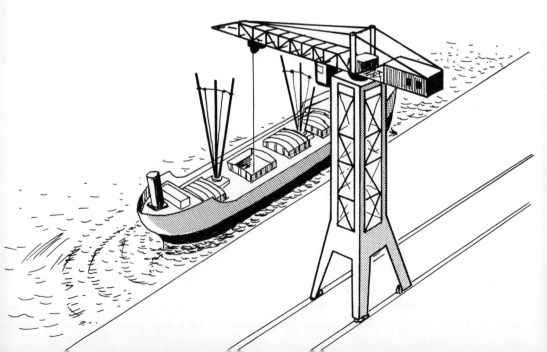

The world's largest floating tower crane is the U.S. Navy's YD-171, over 370 feet tall. It can lift small ships out of the water for repairs and can move about while carrying loads of over 350 tons. The main engines are huge diesels and the winding drums of the winches are ten feet in diameter, carrying over two miles of cable. The crane is controlled from a cab located fifty feet above water level.

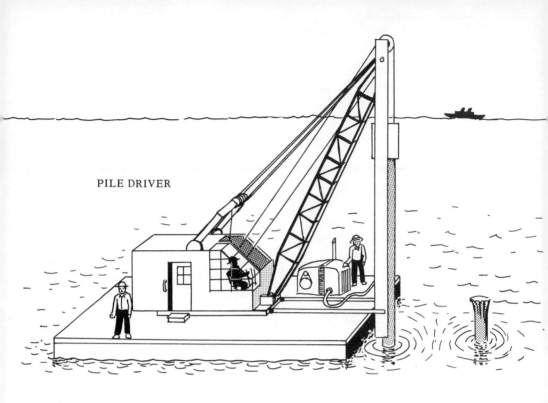

PILE DRIVER

A special kind of crane called a pile driver is used for construction on sandy or wet areas. In these places engineers usually drive long steel, wood, or concrete piles into the ground to provide a firm foundation for the building. These piles are driven by the pile driver, a crane that has a long vertical boom with tracks on which a heavy steel driver runs.

The operator hoists the piling into place against the boom, underneath the driver. The driver, or ram, is raised by compressed air or steam and dropped on the piling. It is raised and dropped again and again, until the piling has been driven deep into the sand.

On large pile drivers, the weight is not only lifted, it is punched down by compressed air, with extra force. Pile drivers mounted on barges drive pilings for bridges, docks, and seawalls.

HELPER FILLS FUEL TANK
ON MOBILE CRANE.

To run cranes (and derricks too) requires a skilled operator, a helper, and sometimes a crew. Usually a man begins work as a helper. He gets his union card and learns the job as he works. He sees that the fuel tank is full and that all the moving parts are clean and well greased. He checks to see that connections are tight and watches for worn or weakened parts that might cause trouble.

Finally, the helper is allowed to take the operator's seat, and then he learns how to work the controls. As he gains experience, he can fill in when regular operators are sick or on vacation. Day by day the helper learns on the job. In time, he is recognized as a full-fledged operator.

Operators of cranes on construction jobs, such as putting up high-rise buildings in crowded cities, must have a quick hand and a sure eye. They must judge heights, distances, and the speed of the load accurately. A good operator can set a ten-ton load on a dime— so gently that nothing is shaken or jarred.

Crane operators, many of whom can operate several kinds of machines, often belong to the Operating Engineers union. Some states and cities also require a license.

When a crane operator cannot see the load clearly, another man called a signalman tells him when to raise, lower, or turn. The signalman always stands where he can see both the load and the operator. He uses hand signals, because he may be too far from the operator to be heard. Hand signals are the same for all kinds of cranes so there is no confusion when more than one kind of crane is used on a job. They are the same even on foreign ships. With hand signals, all crane operators speak the same language.

THE SIGNALMAN STANDS
WHERE HE CAN SEE
BOTH LOAD AND OPERATOR.

HAND SIGNALS USED BY SIGNALMAN

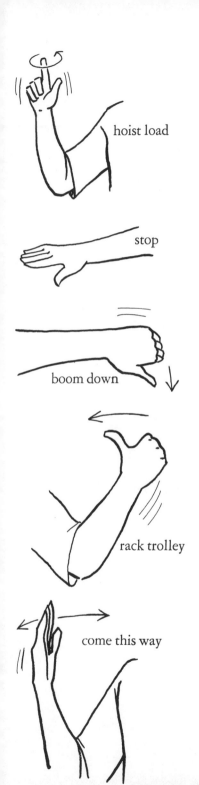

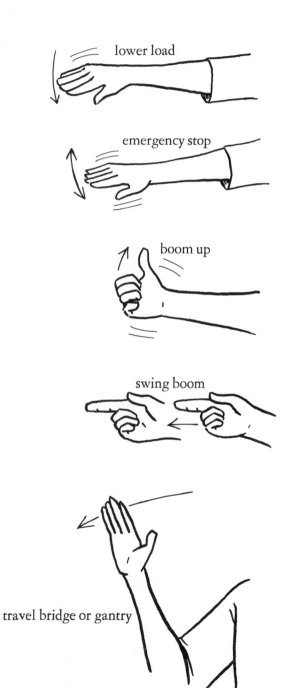

hoist load

lower load

stop

emergency stop

boom down

boom up

rack trolley

swing boom

come this way

travel bridge or gantry

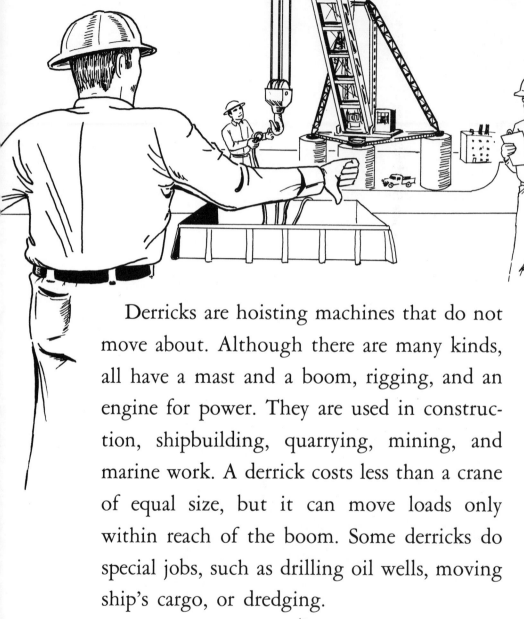

Derricks are hoisting machines that do not move about. Although there are many kinds, all have a mast and a boom, rigging, and an engine for power. They are used in construction, shipbuilding, quarrying, mining, and marine work. A derrick costs less than a crane of equal size, but it can move loads only within reach of the boom. Some derricks do special jobs, such as drilling oil wells, moving ship's cargo, or dredging.

SOME KINDS OF DERRICKS

A-frame derrick
has an A-frame in place of a mast.

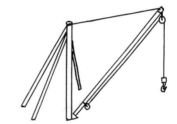

Guy derrick
has a mast supported by guy wires.

Stiffleg derrick
has girders to support a single mast.

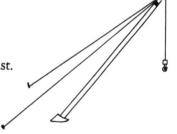

Gin-pole derrick
has guys supporting boom. It has no mast.

Breast derrick
has breast frame to support hoisting rig.
It has no boom.

The mast of a derrick is vertical. It may be a single trestle, an A-frame, or a tripod. A common kind of mast is that of the guy derrick. This mast is held up by four strong guy wires, anchored deep in the ground or to a strong support. On top of the mast, the guy wires are shackled to a steel plate fitting over a heavy pin. This arrangement enables the mast to turn without twisting the guy wires. The bottom of the mast is set on a cross of heavy wood or steel girders.

The boom is hinged near the bottom of the mast, and both parts rotate together. The mast is turned by a large bull wheel or by a long turning bar called a bull stick. The machinery of the derrick is often located in a nearby shed.

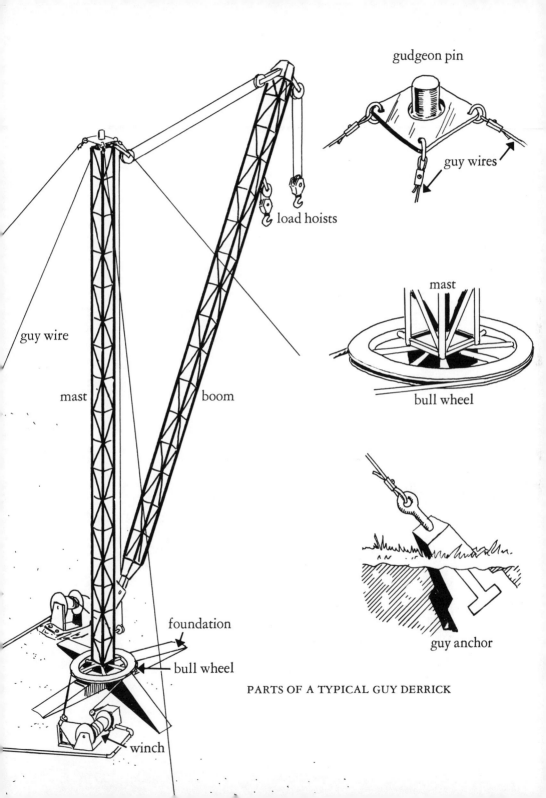

gudgeon pin

guy wires

load hoists

guy wire

mast

boom

mast

bull wheel

foundation

bull wheel

guy anchor

winch

PARTS OF A TYPICAL GUY DERRICK

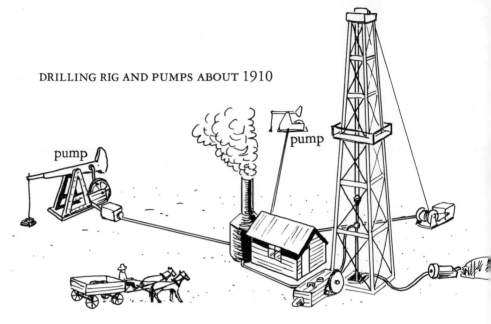

DRILLING RIG AND PUMPS ABOUT 1910

pump

pump

A special kind of derrick, a drilling rig, is used to drill oil wells. These wells go thousands of feet into the earth. As they are dug, the drilling rig raises and lowers the drilling bit of special steel. As the hole gets deeper, the drilling rig also puts a large pipe called a casing into the hole to keep the sides from caving in. Early oil wells had a permanent derrick of wood or steel built over the drilling hole, which stood year after year.

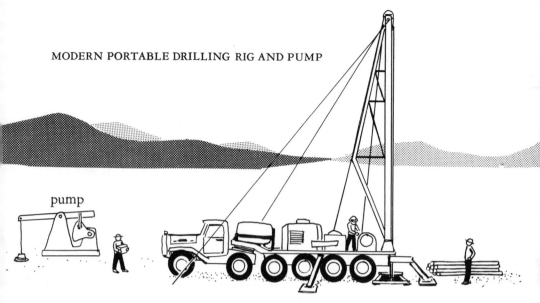

pump

Modern drilling rigs are mounted on great trucks or crawlers that can cross rough country. Besides the derrick framework, the truck also carries the machinery needed to turn the drill and to raise and lower it. When the derrick is in place, it is braced by heavy steel outriggers. After drilling is finished, a pump is fitted to the top of the casing to pump the oil, and the derrick is moved to the next drilling site.

Some oil wells are drilled in shallow parts
of the ocean. The derricks for these wells are
built on floating platforms and towed like
barges to the drilling site. There, huge legs
are pushed down from the platform to the
bottom of the ocean. The hollow legs are

filled with concrete so they will support the derrick more firmly during drilling. The platform is then raised until it is about twenty feet above the water. In addition to holding the derrick, the drilling platform has living quarters for the crew and storage sheds for supplies and equipment. Some even have enough space for a helicopter to land.

Other kinds of derricks are the cargo booms and masts of a freighter. These permanent parts of a ship's rigging are used for moving cargo when there are no quay cranes. The booms are rigged so one extends over the hold and the other over the ship's side.

FREIGHTERS HAVE DERRICKS FOR HANDLING CARGO.

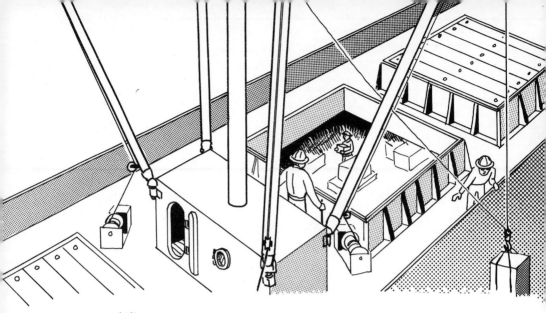

The wire rope from each boom is connected to a single hook. There is a winch for each wire. The winchman works between the winches so he can see down into the hold. A signalman stands at the ship's rail and watches the load when it cannot be seen by the winchman. By working together, the signalman and the winchman raise the load straight up from the hold, swing it over the side, and then drop it down to the waiting crew of stevedores on the dock.

The dredge, used to deepen harbors and channels, is yet another kind of derrick. It is a barge or boat with an A-frame derrick on the forward end. The derrick is used to raise or lower the dredging cutter and the suction pipes that suck up the mud or sand that the cutter digs.

The operator, called a leverman, sits in the wheelhouse atop the forward end of the deckhouse. His controls raise and lower the cutter and move it from side to side. He controls the speed of the cutting and sucking action. In the deckhouse are powerful diesel engines that turn the cutter and run the huge pumps.

DREDGE

Barges with derricks on them are used in marine salvage, bridge building, and other waterfront work. Lighters are smaller barges with derricks, used to move freight about the harbor where the water is not deep enough for large ships to dock. The ship anchors offshore in safe water, and the lighters come out to it. After the cargo is lowered to the decks of the lighters, they move to the dock and unload the cargo with their own small derricks.

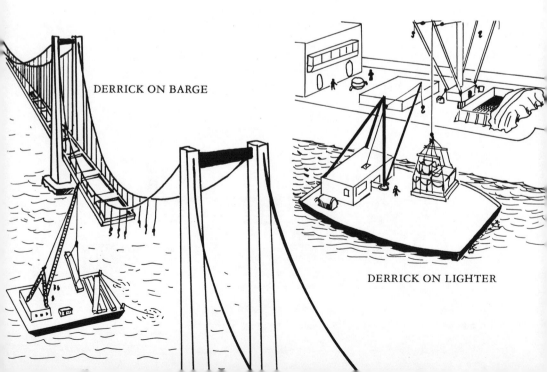

DERRICK ON BARGE

DERRICK ON LIGHTER

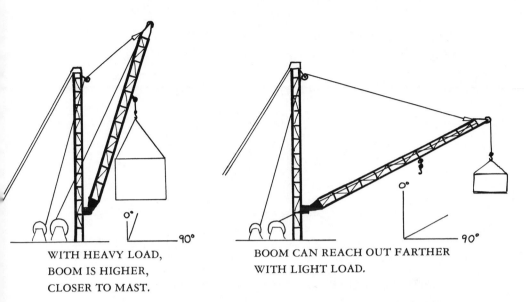

WITH HEAVY LOAD,
BOOM IS HIGHER,
CLOSER TO MAST.

BOOM CAN REACH OUT FARTHER
WITH LIGHT LOAD.

Derricks usually have two or three hooks, located at different places along the boom. The ones closer in to the mast are used for the heavier loads, those at the end of the boom for lighter loads. The reason is that booms can lift more when they are almost straight up. When the boom reaches far out, it cannot lift as much. The operator must use less "stick" if his load is bigger, because the heavy weight might cause the machine to tip.

Seven men usually make up the crew of a common guy derrick, such as one used in heavy construction work. The boom man runs the bull stick and the topping lift that raises or lowers the boom. The signal-man tells when to lift and when to lower by giving hand or bell signals. Two men, who work below, rig the slings on the load. Two more men connect the sling to the hook and see that the load does not swing when it is lifted. These six helpers work closely with the foreman, who operates the winches.

For large hoisting jobs, an engineer may be part of the derrick crew. If a very large block of stone is to be lifted, or a whole section of a ship is to be set in place, the engineer plans the operation so it will go evenly and safely. If such a heavy load slipped, it could ruin the whole job.

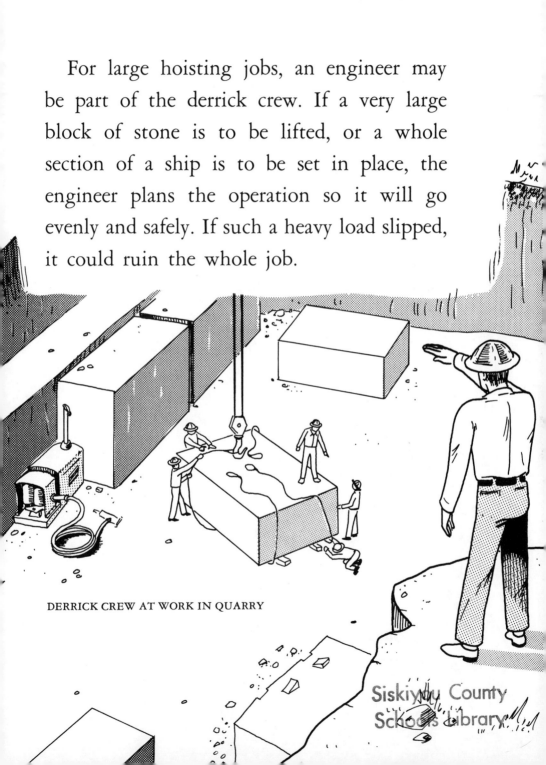

DERRICK CREW AT WORK IN QUARRY

CAPACITIES OF TYPICAL CRANES AND DERRICKS

kind	lifting capacity	span or boom length
bridge crane	over 400 tons	120 feet
quay or dockside crane	20 tons	80 feet
automotive mobile crane	80 tons	100 feet
crawler mobile crane	90 tons	100 feet
building construction tower crane	20 tons	70 feet
heavy tower crane	350 tons	115 feet
stiffleg derrick	30 tons	120 feet
guy derrick	50 tons	120 feet

The men who run hoists, cranes, and derricks do important jobs. Watch how carefully they move heavy materials. Could you work their machines as skillfully? Watch how the operator and his helpers put the load safely just where they want it to go.

Not everyone is quick enough and has good enough control to run a giant crane. Perhaps someday you can be the man who sits at the controls of one of these powerful machines.

INDEX